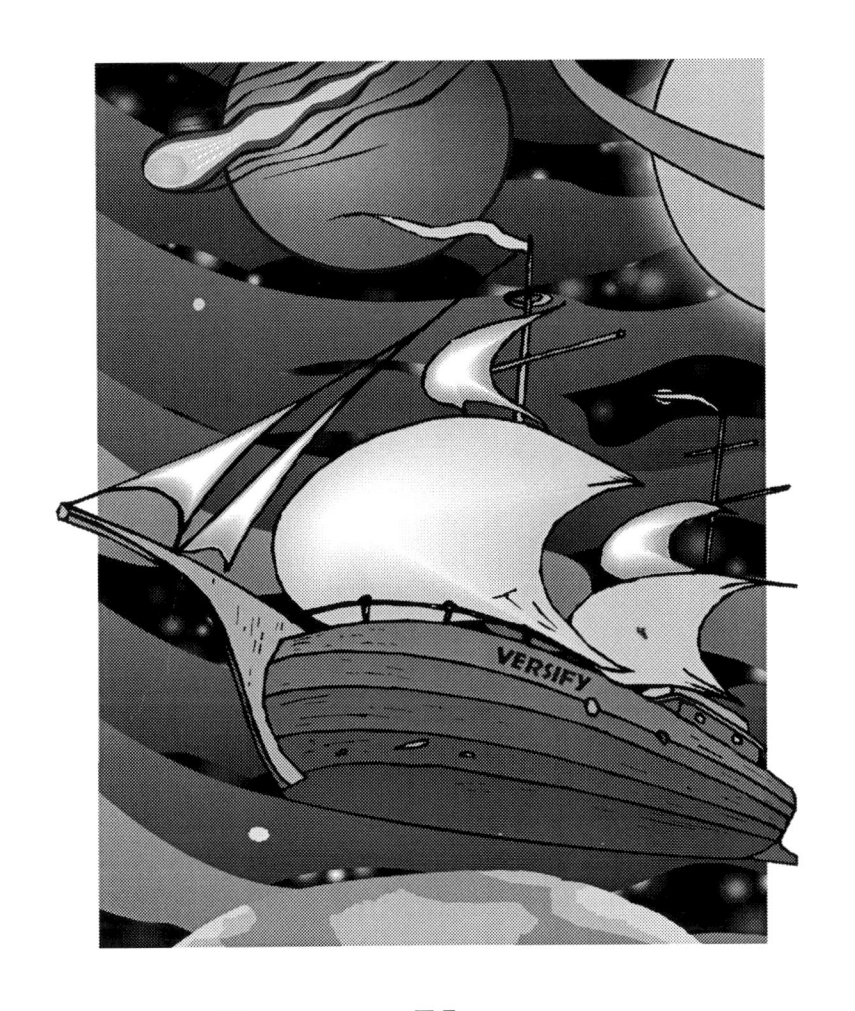

POETIC VOYAGES
RHONDDA CYNON TAFF

Edited by Lucy Jeacock

First published in Great Britain in 2001 by
YOUNG WRITERS
Remus House,
Coltsfoot Drive,
Peterborough, PE2 9JX
Telephone (01733) 890066

All Rights Reserved

Copyright Contributors 2001

HB ISBN 0 75433 150 4
SB ISBN 0 75433 151 2

FOREWORD

Young Writers was established in 1991 with the aim to promote creative writing in children, to make reading and writing poetry fun.

This year once again, proved to be a tremendous success with over 88,000 entries received nationwide.

The Poetic Voyages competition has shown us the high standard of work and effort that children are capable of today. It is a reflection of the teaching skills in schools, the enthusiasm and creativity they have injected into their pupils shines clearly within this anthology.

The task of selecting poems was therefore a difficult one but nevertheless, an enjoyable experience. We hope you are as pleased with the final selection in *Poetic Voyages Rhondda Cynon Taff* as we are.

Contents

	Jessica Griffiths	1
Coed-Y-Lan Primary School		
	Melanie Elizabeth Sandford	1
	Maxine McGlennon	2
	Courtney Elise Pritchard	2
	Carys Elise Oliver	3
	Annabelle Jayne de Frias	3
	Simon Jenkins	4
	Sadie Fosterjohn	4
	Charlotte Edwards	5
	Elizabeth Manjón	5
	Andre Azarian	6
	Laura Brencher	7
	Benjamin Rhys James	7
	Hope Suominen	8
Dinas Junior School		
	Joss Daye	8
	Peter Harris	9
	Alex Carey	10
	Gorgia Chubb	10
	Natasha Bowen	11
	Nicole Bradley	11
	Gary Ryan	12
	Richard Diaper	12
	Daniel Sims	13
	Kieron Robert Davies	14
	Stephanie English	14
	Natalie Jade Williams	15
	Alex Goodwill	16
	Kirsty McDonnell	17
	Rhys Lock	18
	Matthew Ferris	18
	Melanie Jayne Warry	19

Ben James	20
Ashley Jones	20
Sonny Davies	21
Robbie Venables	21
Luke Trembath	22
Lauren Thomas	22
Lauren Jones	23
Natasha Rees	23
Rhys Eshelby	24
Jamie Roberts	24
Amber Jones	25
Natasha Gobey	25
Jordan Jones	26
Abbe Cooper	26
Lauren Williams	27
Kara Griffiths	27
Yazmin Savage	28
Victoria Davies	28
Carwyn Maiden	29
Craig Stead	29
Owain Davies	30
Mitchell Way	31
Kyisha Cooper	32
Thomas Williams	32
Alex James	33
Leanne May	33
Kelly Wilkins	34
Tamara Davies	34
Kayleigh Lloyd	35

Heol-Y-Celyn Primary School

Angela Fiona Hayes	35
Daniel Hayman	36
Lauren Comins	36
Shane Price	37
Sean Howells	37
Nathan Baker	38
Gemma Jones	38

Laura Davies	39
Daniel Hope	39
Dale Llewellyn	40
Bethan Jones	40
Nicola Bridgman	41
Kathleen Sebury	41
Kate Grandfield	42
Michelle Holland	42
Robert Evans	43
Ryan Williams	43
Eliot Newman	44
Matthew Sealey	44
Michaela Evans	45
Cerianne Owen	46
Claire Weston	46
Brian Davies	47
Gabrielle Louise Bunn	48
Laura Rees	48
Jessica Titley	49
Danny Owen	50
Nathan Evans	50
Menna Jane Lucas	51
Louise Walton	51
Amy Louise Jones	52
Thomas Hale	52
Sally Webber	53
Nicky Hopkins	53
Ffion Bunn	54
Joshua Cadwallader	54
Jodie Evans	55
Emma Raison	55
Joshua Hawkins	56
Nadine Rosenberg	56
Sam Fletcher	57
Kieran Williams	57
Daniel Evans	58
Cael Light	59
Rhys Downes	60

Nikki Parfitt	61
Nathan Thomas	62
Rhianydd Jones	63

Llanharan Primary School

Rhiannon Hatter	63
Emma Bradley	64
Jade Allen	64
Rhiannon Davies	65
Ruth Houston	66

Llwyncrwn Primary School

Luke W Davies	66
Sasha Pike	67
Michael Hughes	67
Mathew Smith	68
Scot Taylor	68
Craig Hughes	69
Adam Pincott, Jesse Bees & Scott Ireland	69
Phillip Davies	70
Kelsey Llewellyn	70
Kimberley Homer	71
Carmen Joyce	71
Rachel Leanne Jones	72
Joshua Smith	72
Sarah Bray	73
Tonianne Landsborough	73
Rhys Hain	74
Jade Claridge	74
Sarah Harrison	74
Dale Cox	75
Gemma Evans	75
Wayne Roche	75
Stephanie Lia	76
Bethan Evans	76
Hannah Vaughan	76
Ryan Lee	77
Liam Richards	77

Marc Wingrove	77
Demi Garwood	78
Amy John	78
Shona Pinniger	78
Amy Ferguson	79
Chelsea Jefferies	79
Michael Graham	79
Nia Buckle	80
Charlotte Akers	80
Lucy Daunton	81
Lauren Parry	81
Steven Parry	82
Robert Andrew Powell	82
Lucas Prosser	83
Gemma Baldwin	83
Bethan Griffiths	84
Andrew Burrows	84
Joshua Whitfield	85
Jamie Rees	85
Carly Watkins	86
Gareth Carpenter	86
Ryan Lloyd Palmer	87
Lloyd Morgan	87
Alexandra Jones	88
Laurie Morgan	88
Jonathon Stiff	89
Emma Stafford	89
Tyla Campbell	90
Mathew Binding	90
Victoria Mary Aldred	91
David T J Lacey	91
Samantha Lia	92
Mark Slade	92
Luke Frater	92
Laura Halliday	93
Paul Morris	93
Clare Morgan	94
Andrew Moore	94

Joanne Saunders	94
Ben Thomas	95
Adam Walters	95
Dominic Hickman	95
Steven Perkins	96
Katie Murdoch	96

Llwynpia Primary School

Darren Millard	97
Stacey O'Flaherty	97
Rhys Hopes	98
Jordan Jones	99
Jordan Lee	100
Danielle Gibbs	100
Rhiannan Windsor	101
Jake Jones	101

Maerdy Junior School

Jamie Evans & Bobbie Morris	101
Calvin Ben Williams	102
Emma Louise Kinson	102
Rebecca Podmore	103
Martyn Jones & Ieuan Wilding	103
Philip Jason Thomas & Kyle Osborne	104
Sarah Harris & Chloe Light	104

Penygawsi Primary School

Maria Marling	105
Katherine Houghton	105
Bridie Williams	106
Claire Thomas	106
Alexander Davies	107
Thomas Morgan	107
Francesca Ward	108
Harvey Moisey	108
Matthew Giles	109
Stella Tsouknidas	109
Matthew Evans	110

Rachael Shaw	110
Claire Scowcroft	111
Stuart Wilby	112
Justin Morden	112
Carl Hawkes	113
Kimberley Hawkes	114
Sam Griffiths	114
Bethan Harrison	115
Daniel Halford	115
Jamie Sheppard	116
Sophie Hughes	116
Alexandra Lamb	117
Thomas Wilton	117
Thomas Rees	118
Lauren Bowkett	118

The Poems

BOYS ARE PAINS!

Boys, boys, boys are bad!
They always seem to make girls sad
They drive you up and down the wall
You very often hear them shout 'goal'
Always playing rugby in the yard
Never sorry when they hit us hard
Never see them with their head in a book
Always talking and saying 'Look!'

Jessica Griffiths (8)

LEAVES

Leaves spiral off the trees,
Like a whirlpool in the ocean,
Twirling until you're dizzy.
Crunching when you step on them,
Making you feel the meaning of autumn.
Drifting away to many different places of the globe.
Fluttering like a beautiful butterfly.
With wings the colour of autumn.
The woodland trees have bare branches,
But have a colourful carpet of leaves beneath.
By spring the leaves will be replaced,
And the process will happen again next autumn.

Melanie Elizabeth Sandford (11)
Coed-Y-Lan Primary School

REFUGEES

The streets are cold and lonely
Food is very scarce,
Lucky to get a sheet with holes in
And a cold stone step to sleep on
People stop and stare at you
Kicking you as they go by
You're numb with pain,
Still they push and shove
Bruises all over you,
Nothing but a piece of cloth
To clothe you,
Never knowing whether you'll
See your family again
That's all we need is someone's help
To make a different world

Maxine McGlennon (11)
Coed-Y-Lan Primary School

A VOYAGE

The Giant's Causeway is dirty, dark and dusty.
The waves are crashing on the rocks like thunder.
I imagine glistening gold treasure
Scattered among the rocks.
The noise is like elephants' feet trampling over the rocks.
I feel scared.

Courtney Elise Pritchard (7)
Coed-Y-Lan Primary School

A VOYAGE

I discovered a lost land called Cave Land where there are lots of caves.
There are also cave paintings on the walls.
It smells like a dead, slimy snake.
There is also a volcano which explodes every year, like thunder hitting the sea.
There is coloured sand and volcanic rocks on the beach.
On the beach is hidden treasure.
You can also catch fish in the sea on the beach.
The river leads you to a red castle on the other side of the river.
The corridors are creepy and crooked.
The doors are noisy and there are ghosts inside.

Carys Elise Oliver (8)
Coed-Y-Lan Primary School

THE SCARY CASTLE

The red castle is old and scary.
It looks like a crown.
The corridor walls are like slimy, slippery slugs.
In the cupboard are very big spider's webs.
On the walls are cave paintings.
In the underground caves.

The sea is crashing on the red castle with steam.
It goes to the Giant's Causeway.
It is as long as a giraffe's neck with hundreds of stones.

Annabelle Jayne de Frias (8)
Coed-Y-Lan Primary School

HIBERNATION

Animals bolt around,
To find their valuable provisions,
Like pirates searching for golden treasure,
Day after day,
As they poke around for grub,
Like a skunk,
Nuts, bugs and corn,
The ingredients of hibernation.

Animals scan the forest,
For twigs and leaves,
For their snugly hideout,
The tiring searching goes on,
For the second ingredient of hibernation.

Simon Jenkins (11)
Coed-Y-Lan Primary School

A VOYAGE

The red castle is old, murky and dark,
Its corridors are cold, creepy and calm,
With slime on the walls.
You can hear faint cries
And the sea crashing against the walls like a serpent's tongue.
In the pitch black you can hear booms of volcanoes all around,
You can smell the horrible smell from the dungeons,
And the hay which they used to sleep on.

Sadie Fosterjohn (8)
Coed-Y-Lan Primary School

FLICKERING LIGHT

That loud banging noise,
Pets run and hide under the bed,
Thunder bangs against windows,
Whilst little children scream,
Lightning is a *flickering light*

Electricity flickers on and off,
Candles burn,
As we creep around,
Telephone wires are dead,
As lightning travels across the hillside,

Don't go out when there's a storm!

Charlotte Edwards (10)
Coed-Y-Lan Primary School

AUTUMN

The rain is beating on the ground,
Like a hammer bashing in a nail,
The thunder is approaching,
Like a giant's long groan,
The leaves are blowing everywhere,
Like a blizzard of colours,
The animals don't dare come out,
They stay in their houses as still as statues,
The lightning comes,
It nearly cracks the mountain in half,
The trees are stripped bare,
Like sheep without wool.

Elizabeth Manjón (10)
Coed-Y-Lan Primary School

DRIVEN OUT

Suddenly I am not allowed to live with my family,
What is going to happen to me?
The Nazi men just threw us in a cattle truck,
Like we are just a piece of rubbish,
I'm so angry,
I wish I could round the Germans up and shoot them all,
This place that I'm living is disgusting,
We have no food or drink,
We are lucky to get a crumb,
Sleeping in my own excrement,
Packed together with no room to move,
My family are probably dead,
Just thrown on a pile of bodies,
I'll just be killed like the rest of them,
rounded up and gassed,
I don't see why we should be treated like this,
Why should we be killed if our nose is too big or if we are too old?
I look like a skeleton, you can see every bone in my body as I have
               no flesh,
I must see my family,
I need to know if they are dead or alive?
Soon it will be my turn to be butchered, like a pig on a farm,
I hope I see the sunlight again,
But now I never will.

Andre Azarian (11)
Coed-Y-Lan Primary School

FRIGHTENING AUTUMN STORMS

The sky turns a frightening black in the flicker of an eyelid,
It is chained to its place until the storm is over,
The rain bashes against the ground like the sound of a hammer,
The thunder is as penetrating and disrupting as a chemical
                lab exploding,
Lightning dashes across the sky in a sequence as it comes closer,
The animals scamper and scurry across the fields for safety,
The sea nearby becomes turbulent,
As it slams against the coarse rocks,
The hailstones slam against the ground one after another,
Suddenly the lightning stops,
Closely followed by the thunder,
The sky turns blue once more,
As the animals return to the field.

Laura Brencher (10)
Coed-Y-Lan Primary School

A FIELDMOUSE IN A CORNFIELD

A fieldmouse creeps through the damp cornfield,
Searching the ground for a golden grain of corn,
He carries on through the cold soil,
The wheat arches over the tiny mouse like a wave over the sand,
The field mouse stands on his hind legs sniffing the clear, fresh air,
Swifts and swallows on their migration journey sweep across the sky,
The wheat is a maze made by the giant,
Its golden fur ruffles as the wind brushes over the fieldmouse,
The grain is found as the mouse speeds across the ground and picks
                it up,
Back over the cornfield goes the little fieldmouse with its golden grain
                of corn.

Benjamin Rhys James (11)
Coed-Y-Lan Primary School

THE SILVER SHIP

The ship appears with a clash,
As the ship condenses out of the frozen dusky mist,
The wind smashing against the silver ship.
The ship floats in mid-air,
While the fog separates,
The wind crashes against the ship,
The roaring sea underneath the ship,
Bashes against the cobbled stones,
The strong sea hits the slow-motive ship,
As it leaves the cold frozen air.

Hope Suominen (10)
Coed-Y-Lan Primary School

OUR COUNTRY WALES

W is for Welsh which some of us speak,
A is for our anthem, the Land of my Fathers,
L is for leek, an emblem of Wales,
E is for etifeddiaeth - the heritage of which we are so proud,
S is for Strady Park, the home pitch of the Scarlets.
  This tells us of our wonderful Wales
  The glorious land of valley and song.

Joss Daye (8)
Dinas Junior School

IF

If I had the teeth of a tiger,
I could tear my enemies to shreds
And crunch their bones to dust.

If I had the wings of an eagle,
I could fly round the world
And explore every country.

If I had the arms of an octopus,
I could do my homework twice as fast
And finish before anyone in the class.

If I had the memory of an elephant,
I could memorise all my spelling words
And get a hundred percent.

If I had the body of a whale,
I would swim in the Olympics
And win the world gold medal for swimming.

If I had the body of a horse,
I would gallop all over the mountains
And lie in the hay.

If I had the arms of a monkey,
I would swing around the park
And look down from a tall lamp post.

Peter Harris (9)
Dinas Junior School

IF

If I had the teeth of a tiger
I could tear my enemies to shreds
And crunch their bones to dust.

If I had the memory of an elephant
I could memorise my spelling words
And get 100% each time.

If I had the legs of an octopus
I could do more than one thing at a time
And win the underwater Olympics.

If I had the string of a spider
I could spin a web in five seconds
And then rest and wait for bugs all day.

If I had the gills of a fish
I could swim into the Atlantic Ocean
And explore the Titanic.

Alex Carey (10)
Dinas Junior School

CYMRU

C is for canu or singing to you,
Y is for Ysgol, our school we go to.
M is for 'Mae hen wlad fy nhadau,' our anthem of song,
R is for rugby we play all day long,
U is for Urdd we take part in each year.
   Croeso I Gymru
     Is what we like to hear.

Gorgia Chubb (9)
Dinas Junior School

THE BEACH

Walk along the beach,
Maybe you will see a bottle with a letter inside it,
A person playing tennis on the golden light sand,
Or children swimming in the big, bright sea.

Walk along the beach,
Maybe you will see a woman rubbing suncream into her skin,
Or maybe a girl making a big sandcastle,
Or maybe a mermaid sitting on the high grey rocks.

Walk along the beach,
Even if there's a ball rolling across the sea,
Even if there's only a man playing football,
Even if there's people walking across the sand.

Walk along the beach,
At least it is sunny.

Natasha Bowen (11)
Dinas Junior School

CHRISTMAS TIME

I love Christmas
With shiny lights
And Christmas pudding
And lovely Christmas balls
Yes I love Christmas.
Christmas Time
I love Christmas
With the Christmas stockings
And Christmas presents
And the Christmas tree
Yes I love Christmas.

Nicole Bradley (9)
Dinas Junior School

IF

If I had the teeth of a tiger,
I could tear my enemies to shreds,
And crunch their forms into dust.

If I had the wings of a bird,
I could fly high up in the sky,
And above the soft white clouds.

If I had the gills of a fish,
I could swim all around the ocean's bed,
And see all the beautiful fish.

If I had the legs of a spider,
I could scamper all over the wall,
And walk upside down.

If I had the electricity of an eel,
I could electrocute other fish in the sea,
And recharge with other eels.

If I had the smallness of a mouse,
I could creep and nibble through cheese,
And be chased by cats.

Gary Ryan (10)
Dinas Junior School

THE DARK WOODS

Down in the dark woods,
If you look carefully,
You can see,
A grizzly bear sleeping,
A pack of wolves running after a badger,
A hunter shooting rabbits
And some owls getting food.

Down in the dark woods,
If you listen carefully,
You can hear,
The hoot of an owl,
The bark of a pack of hounds,
The howl of a wolf,
The sound of the flowing stream,
And the bang of a gun.

Richard Diaper (9)
Dinas Junior School

IF

If I had the teeth of a tiger,
I could tear my enemies to shreds
And crunch their bones to dust.

If I had the memory of an elephant,
I could remember all of my spelling words
And have a hundred percent.

If I had the wings of a dove,
I could spread my wings
And bring peace to the world.

If I had the gills of a fish,
I could search for lost treasure
And see different types of underwater life.

If I had the arms of a monkey,
I could swing from branch to branch
And win every game of hide and seek.

If I had the legs of an ostrich,
I could win every race entered
And win the London Marathon.

Daniel Sims (10)
Dinas Junior School

THE DOOR

Go and open the door,
maybe outside there's
a member of the Welsh Rugby Club
a queen come for some tea and some biscuits
or a Porsche with David Beckham going to take me for a ride.

Go and open the door,
maybe there's a mouse on a scooter
or there's a dog chasing a cat
or there's a cat chasing a mouse.

Go and open the door
even if there's only
nothing there to see.

Even if there's only
a cat waiting to eat the mouse.

Even if
the dog is waiting outside to chase the cat.

Go and open the door.

Keiron Robert Davies (10)
Dinas Junior School

IF

If I had the teeth of a tiger
I could tear my enemies to shreds
And crunch their bones into dust.

If I had the memory of an elephant
I could memorise my spelling words
And get 100%.

If I had the legs of an octopus
I could do eight things at the same time
And swim the ocean depths.

If I had the wings of a dove
I would spread peace all over the world
And everyone would live in harmony.

Stephanie English (9)
Dinas Junior School

THE DOOR

Go and open the door,
Maybe outside there's
A kangaroo jumping up and down
A rainbow with skittles falling onto the ground
Or some money falling from the sky.

Go and open the door,
Maybe there's a person on a motorbike skidding in the moors
Or leaves blowing off the trees
Or a boxing match in the garden.

Go and open the door,
Even if there's only a leaf blowing on the floor.

Even if there's only
A postman putting letters in the boxes.

Even if there is nothing there.
Go and open the door.

Natalie Jade Williams (10)
Dinas Junior School

IF

If I had the teeth of a tiger,
I could tear my enemies to shreds
And crunch their bones to dust.

If I had the wings of a dove,
I could fly to exotic places
And bask in the sun.

If I had the trunk of an elephant,
I could smell beautiful foods from everywhere
And pick fruit from high places.

If I had the legs of a centipede,
I could join the Olympics
And spend a fortune on boots.

If I had the gills of a fish
I could go deep under the Atlantic Ocean searching for wrecks
And look for hidden silver on the seabed.

If I had the body of a bull,
I could charge around my field
And make my enemies run away.

If I had the roar of a lion,
I could make all the animals quake
And treat me as King of the jungle.

If I had the speed of a cheetah,
I could chase my enemies
And kill them for my food.

If I had the smallness of an ant,
I could go into the kitchen through tiny cracks
And raid the cupboards.

Alex Goodwill (9)
Dinas Junior School

IF

If I had the teeth of a tiger,
I could tear my enemies to shreds
And crunch their bones to dust.

If I had the wings of a bird,
I could fly up in the sky
And spy on the rest of the world.

If I had the brain of a fox,
I could hide in the barn
And eat all the chickens.

If I had the legs of a spider,
I could run very fast
And spin a web of silk.

If I had the neck of a giraffe,
I could reach the top of the trees
And eat the green, luscious leaves.

If I had the bite of a snake,
I could hide in the grass
And strike unexpectedly on unsuspecting mice.

If I had the gills of a fish,
I could swim the depths of the ocean
And explore all kinds of sea life.

Kirsty McDonnell (10)
Dinas Junior School

THE DOOR

Go and open the door
Maybe outside there's
A football pitch with David Beckham scoring against Liverpool
A limousine waiting outside my door for me
Or a horse galloping across the field

Go and open the door
Maybe there's a man with giraffe legs
Or a snowy day so we don't have to go to school
Or a TV series of the Simpsons

Go and open the door
Even if there's only
An apple rolling down the street
Even if there's only
A leaf flying silently in the air
Even if
There's a dog talking to a mouse
Go and open the door

Rhys Lock (10)
Dinas Junior School

CHRISTMASTIME

I love Christmas
With Santa on his way
And Christmas decorations
And the beautiful soft smell
I love Christmas

I love Christmas
With toys in my stocking
And the children in the soft snow
I love Christmas

Matthew Ferris (8)
Dinas Junior School

THE BEACH

Walk along the beach,
Maybe there's a mermaid sitting on a rock brushing her long hair,
A little puppy might be chasing after his tail,
Or there might be a happy child riding on a donkey.

Walk along the beach,
Maybe there might be men or women surfing across the sea,
Or there might be lots of children having fun,
Or people catching a sun tan from the golden sun.

Walk along the beach,
Even if there's only the soft golden sand,
Even if there's only a dolphin jumping into the air,
Even if there's no one out there.

Walk along the beach,
At least there's the light blue sea.

Melanie Jayne Warry (10)
Dinas Junior School

THE BEACH

Walk along the beach,
Maybe there's a little king claiming his sandcastle
A big wave with a little fish inside,
Or a big hole with children inside.

Walk along the beach,
Maybe there's a person as happy as can be,
Or a scuba waiting to be used,
Or a big hand pouring water into the sea.

Walk along the beach,
Even if there's only an isolated beach with smooth sea,
Even if there's no one, no movement,
Even if there's nothing to do at all.

Walk along the beach,
At least we'll get a tan.

Ben James (11)
Dinas Junior School

SAINT DAVID

Saint David is the patron saint of Wales,
He was born in Pembrokeshire,
His father's name was Sandde and his mother's name was Non,
When David was born a storm was all round
But on David and his mother and father sunlight shone.

When David went to school, his teacher's name was Paulinus,
Paulinus was blind until David touched his eyelids.
Then he was able to see again.

Ashley Jones (10)
Dinas Junior School

THE BEACH

Walk along the beach.

Maybe there's a mermaid flattered because everyone adores her,
a lovely, cheerful, blue sky and the sun shining like a fire ball,
or a fisherman getting worried that he isn't catching any fish.

Walk along the beach.

Maybe there are shells (shining glamourously)
or people satisfied about the beach's condition,
or rare seagulls flapping their outstanding wings.

Walk along the beach.

Even if there's only water lying peacefully on the beach.

Walk along the beach.

At least you'll have some peace on your own.

Sonny Davies (10)
Dinas Junior School

SAINT DAVID

When Saint David was born it was a stormy day,
A teacher called Paulinus was blind,
But David touched his eyes and he could see,
Later in his life he made miracles happen
And everybody saw,
Ever since the hill rose,
All the people were happy,
Saint David was glad he could help people.

Robbie Venables (9)
Dinas Junior School

THE BEACH

Walk along the beach.
Maybe there's a dolphin with a ball on his nose,
a donkey giving people a ride,
or women on sunbeds.

Walk along the beach.
Maybe there's some nude people on the sand,
or there's a blue sky with the sun in it,
or there's a group of boys playing with a beach ball.

Walk along the beach.
Even if there's only some footprints on the beach,
even if there's only black rocks in the sea,
even if there's just a man walking there.
Walk along the beach,
at least you'll see the sea.

Luke Trembath (10)
Dinas Junior School

GLEAM

Gleam will jump, land with a bump
And trot round the field
Clip-clop, clip
Tommy on his back, 'Gleam, go faster.'
Tommy falls off
Gleam canters to his stable.

Gleam, Gleam, gallop through the village trees
Jump over that jump
Oops you've landed with a thump
And you've got a lump on your nose.

Lauren Thomas (7)
Dinas Junior School

THE BEACH

Walk along the beach,
Maybe there's a mermaid sitting on the rocks with her long hair,
A Punch and Judy show with loads of people watching it,
Or maybe you might have a go on the pedal boats,
Walk along the beach.

Maybe you'll see people building sandcastles,
Or people playing with beach balls in the sea,
Or kids in a long queue buying ice cream,
Walk along the beach.

Even if there's only footsteps in the sand,
Even if there's only shells on the floor,
Even if seaweed is tied to your legs,
Walk along the beach.

At least you'll catch the sun.

Lauren Jones (10)
Dinas Junior School

SAINT DAVID

Saint David was born a long time ago.
A boy who grew into a good man.
In the night there was a big storm.
There was a chapel that was safe.

David helped his blind teacher, Paulinus.
He touched his eyes and he could see.
He became the patron saint of Wales
And we celebrate every year.

Natasha Rees (9)
Dinas Junior School

THE BEACH

Walk along the beach,
Maybe there's a donkey with a child having fun,
A group of friends playing volleyball,
Or a shark being nice to someone.

Walk along the beach,
Maybe there's a mermaid bushing her hair,
Or Baywatch lifeguards running towards you,
Walk along the beach.

Even if there's only shells in the sea,
Even if there's only a pile of sand,
Even if there's only somebody sunbathing,
Walk along the beach.

At least there will be water.

Rhys Eshelby (11)
Dinas Junior School

SAINT DAVID

S   aint David was the son of Non, his mother and Sandde, his father,
A fter David was born he performed a miracle,
I   njured man called Paulinus was blind, he could see again.
N on, his mother, ran away from her enemies,
T here was a man called Credeg, who was the father of Sandde.

D avid was born many years ago,
A fter he had grown up he became the patron saint of Wales,
V is for David who lived a very long time ago,
I   f you would celebrate this day,
D avid was a good man who performed lots of miracles.

Jamie Roberts (9)
Dinas Junior School

THE DOOR

Go and open the door,
Maybe outside there's
A garden full of beautiful flowers,
A tree with nice red apples on it,
Or a rainbow with skittles falling from it.

Go and open the door,
Maybe there's a limousine waiting for you,
Or a rugby player waiting to take you for dinner,
Or a football player waiting to take you for a drink.

Go and open the door,
Even if there's only
A leaf blowing across the garden,
Even if there's only
A bird singing in a tree,
Even if
There's an elephant drinking out of the pond,
Go and open the door.

Amber Jones (11)
Dinas Junior School

SPORT

S is for soccer which is fun to play,
P is for pool which is full of water,
O is for Olympics with jumping and running,
R is for rugby which is a rough game,
T is for tennis which you play with a racquet.

Natasha Gobey (9)
Dinas Junior School

IF

If I had the wings of an eagle,
I could fly up high in the sky
And swoop over mountains and oceans.

If I had the fangs of a tarantula,
I could catch my own prey
And climb up trees to make webs.

If I had the gills of a fish,
I could swim in the depths of the ocean
And find a sunken galleon.

If I had the legs of a millipede,
I could do all my homework at once
And run to school faster.

If I had the nose of a dog
I could smell things from miles away
And know where people were hiding.

Jordan Jones (9)
Dinas Junior School

THE WOMBAT

The wombat lives across the seas,
Among the far Antipodes.
He may exist on nuts and berries,
Or then again, on missionaries!
His little habits precludes
Conclusive of his little moods.
I could not call the wombat
Any form of a combat.

Abbe Cooper (8)
Dinas Junior School

BUBBLEGUM

Out in the yard we have fun,
Eating and blowing bubblegum.
Bubbles big, bubbles small,
Eating gum for one and all.

When the bell goes, in we come,
In my mouth there's bubblegum.
In our class we have a bin,
So I can drop my bubblegum in.

When the bell goes at twenty to four,
There's no school then anymore.
When I go home and have my tea,
Lovely bubblegum waits for me!

Lauren Williams (9)
Dinas Junior School

CHRISTMAS!

I love Christmas
    With Santa on his way
And the sparkling shiny lights
    Yes I love Christmas.

I love Christmas
    With lovely decorations
And bright lights
    Yes I love Christmas.

Kara Griffiths (7)
Dinas Junior School

THE DARK WOODS

Down in the dark woods,
If you look carefully
You can see,
Squirrels scampering,
Rabbits twitching,
Birds fluttering,
Hedgehogs hibernating
And foxes hunting.

Down in the dark woods,
If you listen carefully
You can hear,
Owls hooting,
Leaves rustling,
Conkers crashing,
Birds twittering,
And bears grunting.

Yazmin Savage (9)
Dinas Junior School

SAINT DAVID

Saint David lived in Pembrokeshire
He is the patron saint of Wales
Every March the first, the day he died,
The girls wear Welsh costumes
And the boys wear Welsh rugby shirts,
We're glad to celebrate this good man.

Victoria Davies (9)
Dinas Junior School

CHRISTMASTIME

I love Christmas
with the glittery paper
and the lovely presents
and I like the stockings
Yes I love Christmas.

I love Christmas
with my mother and father
and my brother too
and I go to bed excitedly
Yes I love Christmas.

I love Christmas
with waking up early
and opening my presents
Yes I love Christmas.

Carwyn Maiden (9)
Dinas Junior School

CHRISTMAS

See
See the flashing lights.
See the lovely angel on top of the tree.
See the snow falling from the sky.
See the little robin flying over our heads.

Hear
Hear the choir singing.
Hear Santa landing on the roof.
Hear people saying Merry Christmas.
Hear the Christmas bells ringing.

Craig Stead (8)
Dinas Junior School

IF

If I had the teeth of a shark,
I could tear my enemies to shreds
And crunch their bones to dust.

If I had the wings of a bird,
I could fly very high
And touch the tops of the clouds.

If I had the legs of a spider,
I could crawl up and down things
And spin a web of silk.

If I had the legs of a centipede,
I could run fast and win the Olympics
And crawl across the meadow grass.

If I had the fins of a fish,
I could beat Ian Thorpe
And be the swimming champion.

If I had the neck of a giraffe
I could reach the tops of trees
And eat all the luscious leaves.

If I had the brain of a fox,
I could catch all the mice
And eat lots of chickens.

If I had the ears of an elephant,
I could hear from far and near
And listen to the stream flowing.

If I had the mouth of a caterpillar,
I could eat lots of leaves
And also eat the stems.

Owain Davies (10)
Dinas Junior School

CHRISTMAS

See the beautiful flashing trees on Christmas Day
And all of the presents under the tree.
See the snowflakes falling from the sky.
See the fascinating decorations.
See the children playing in the snow.
See the little robin flying over our heads.

Hear the Christmas paper rattle.
Hear Santa coming down the chimney.
Hear the Christmas bells, ding dong ding.
Hear the Christmas carols singing at the door.
Hear the bells on Santa's sleigh.

Smell the lovely Christmas food.
Smell the minty candles.
Smell the wax burning.
Smell the tasty chicken.
Smell the beautiful yummy chicken.

Taste the lovely food.
Taste the beautiful chicken.
Taste the Christmas chocolate.
Taste the beautiful advent calendar.
Taste the beautiful sweets.

Mitchell Way (8)
Dinas Junior School

SAINT DAVID

Many years ago a baby boy was born,
His name was David,
He was born in Chapel Non,
The lightning crashed but the sun still shone.

David was a great man,
He was good to many people,
He knew many miracles,
The best miracle he performed was when
He made his teacher see again.

David became our Patron Saint,
We celebrate on March the first,
We dress in costumes and sing Welsh songs,
We wear the bright yellow daffodil.

Kyisha Cooper (9)
Dinas Junior School

ST DAVID

David was born in Chapel Non
And he was the grandson of the prince of Credig,
Very long ago he was a saint and a good man,
In a very bad storm David was born,
David was a helper and we celebrate on March the first.

Thomas Williams (9)
Dinas Junior School

CHRISTMAS

I love Christmas
With Santa on his way
And snowflakes falling from the sky
And the children playing in the snow
Yes I love Christmas.

I love Christmas
With the angel on top of the tree
And the sparkling shiny lights
I'm going to bed early
Yes I love Christmas.

Alex James (9)
Dinas Junior School

CHRISTMAS

I love Christmas
With Rudolph's shiny nose,
And the beautiful shining presents,
And Christmas decorations around the window
Yes I love Christmas.

I love Christmas
With Santa on his way,
And Christmas decorations,
And the children playing in the snow
Yes I love Christmas.

Leanne May (7)
Dinas Junior School

SAINT DAVID

S aint David is special in every way
A nd he is special because he helped Paulinus
I f you are Welsh, we will celebrate with a fete
N on, who was David's mother, was also very special
T he church that David was born in is called Chapel Non

D ragon is the emblem of Wales,
A ll the people celebrate and cheer,
V ery long time ago Saint David was kind,
I f you are from Wales you would dress up,
D avid was a very good man.

Kelly Wilkins (9)
Dinas Junior School

SAINT DAVID

Saint David is the patron saint of Wales
He was born in a chapel in Pembrokeshire
When he was born it was thundering and lightning
But on his cottage, the sun shone.

On Saint David's Day, we sing Welsh songs
We wear Welsh clothes and daffodils
We win competitions and shout hip hip hooray
We are happy on this day.

Tamara Davies (9)
Dinas Junior School

SAINT DAVID

Our Saint Dewi Sant is the patron of Wales.
A man called Paulinus was blind until Dewi touched his eyes,
Non was Dewi Sant's mother,
On Saint David's Day we wear Welsh rugby shirts,
We have photos taken and dress up,
And celebrate Saint David's Day.

Kayleigh Lloyd (9)
Dinas Junior School

SWEETS

Sweets, sweets are so good
Sweets, sweets are so sweet
Sweets, sweets are to eat

Sweets, sweets are everywhere
Sweets, sweets are nice to eat
Sweets, sweets are fun to buy
Sweets, sweets are fun to suck
Sweets, sweets are nearly here
Sweets, sweets are nearly
Sweets, sweets are Christmastime
Sweets, sweets are New Year's Day
Sweets, sweets are a dawn of a day
Sweets, sweets on friendship day
Sweets, sweets make you fat
Sweets, sweets make you sweet.

Angela Fiona Hayes (9)
Heol-Y-Celyn Primary School

THE MAN IN THE ROCKET

The man in the rocket's name was Crockett,
Landed on Jupiter,
Saw girls getting even more stupider,
Went to Mars to find some cars,
One was a Granada,
Went to Pluto,
To play a game of Cluedo,
Went to the Milky Way,
To get some chocolate,
Finally went to the Sun to have some fun,
And never came back to Earth again.

Daniel Hayman (9)
Heol-Y-Celyn Primary School

MORNING

While you are snoring
The sun will be calling
Get up, get out of bed

While you are snoring
The sun is dawning
Up over the hills

While you are snoring
The sun will be making the morning
While you're getting out of bed.

Lauren Comins (10)
Heol-Y-Celyn Primary School

WWF

There was a champion in WWF.
He fought and fought
all the rest.
He's quite good but not
the best.
He was in this first blood match
he thought it was easy
so he slept.

He won the title
and then he wept.
His name was Kurt
he's an Olympic twerp.
Edge and Christian
were stable
But the Dudleys put them through
a table.

Vince McMahon tried to be fair
but Kurt's losing his hair.
He took his anger out on
Rock but he just said, 'Stop.'

Shane Price (10)
Heol-Y-Celyn Primary School

SPACE

Space is very far
You can't get there in a car
It has nine planets in the sky
They are very high
It is very black
'Whoops!' I can't find my way back.

Sean Howells (10)
Heol-Y-Celyn Primary School

MY SCHOOL

My school is cool,
I think it's great.
There are some things I love
And some things I hate.

I love doing Maths
and I love PE.
But one thing I don't like
Is boring RE.

I have many friends
For me to play,
And working together
Makes a special day.

Nathan Baker (8)
Heol-Y-Celyn Primary School

ANIMALS

Animals are everywhere
Never seen a polar bear
I've seen a cat
But not seen a bat
I've seen a rat
But not a gnat
Animals are anywhere

Gemma Jones (9)
Heol-Y-Celyn Primary School

A NIGHT WITH YOU

As I see the moon,
Glitter in your eyes,
I smile.

As I hear the wind,
Blow your whiskers smoothly,
I shiver.

As I brush your fur,
You purr,
Then smile.

As I put you to bed,
You lay,
And sleep.

Laura Davies (10)
Heol-Y-Celyn Primary School

THE JUNGLE

Down in the jungle
Where the lions roar
And the monkeys swing
From tree to tree
I like to watch
The hippos bathing in a mud bath
And ride up high on the back of an elephant
And see the giraffes stretch up high
To reach the tallest leaves.

Daniel Hope (8)
Heol-Y-Celyn Primary School

SNOW

Snow has come again
It gleams all over the cars
It is stuck in the gutter.

The roads are blocked
Because they are covered in snow!
Some people could
Not get
Their fires on.

Children play in snow!
They have snowballs.
They fight!
They dress up warm.
They have hats on and gloves on.

Dale Llewellyn (10)
Heol-Y-Celyn Primary School

DOLPHINS

Dolphins swimming in the sea
Playing games like you and me
Dancing, swimming, having fun
Singing all day in the sun.
Splash and dash, playing ball
Throwing it back and forth
Flapping their fins
Waving goodbye
Singing rhymes
One at a time.

Bethan Jones (8)
Heol-Y-Celyn Primary School

LIFE OF A ROBIN

I am a robin,
a bird of snow
my little red breast
is all aglow.

I perch on a branch
and wipe the snow from each feather
as I watch the snow gently
fall on the heather.

The grass is covered
in a white sort of powder
and icicles hang
from each flower.

Nicola Bridgeman (10)
Heol-Y-Celyn Primary School

SPACE

Space is very far away
I'd like to go there some day.
Catch the moon
Until noon
I might meet aliens soon.
Who knows what's up there?
I'll just sit and stare!

Kathleen Sebury (8)
Heol-Y-Celyn Primary School

THE FROSTY DAY

The frosty winter day, everyone asleep
even a mouse
everyone wakes opening the curtains,
the powdered hoar frost lay
all over the ground.
Babies crawling up and down
not wondering what's happening
putting Tigger's paws on the ground.

The snow is falling fast
the tender loving cat sleeps by the fire
on his cuddly mat
no one there to disturb him.

Only Jack Frost can see him
he looks in and sees a little cat
sleeping on the mat.

Kate Grandfield (11)
Heol-Y-Celyn Primary School

COLOURS

Colours are bright
Like pink, black and white
Green and blue are beautiful too
Purple and grey are not far away
I see lots of colours every day

Michelle Holland (8)
Heol-Y-Celyn Primary School

FROST ALL OVER

We play rugby in the frost
It is cold in shorts!
Scrapes and scratches
All over.

The park is slippery
Children playing on
Swing and slide.

Children crying in
The streets,
The road is slippery today.

It was so like
A winter wonderland
With frost all over.

The winter is over
Until next time!

Robert Evans (11)
Heol-Y-Celyn Primary School

THE SMALL BROWN BEAR

The small brown bear
fishes
with strong paws
he wishes
he could catch
his favourite dishes
a trout or a salmon yum-yum!

Ryan Williams (8)
Heol-Y-Celyn Primary School

MY UNCLE

My uncle is very tall,
Almost as solid as a wall.
My uncle will argue even when he is wrong,
Although he is very strong.
He has *very* big muscles,
And when shopping he hustles and bustles.
When he was younger he had a lot of hair,
He looked similar to a grizzly bear.
My uncle is always full of fun and happy,
Apart from when he changes a baby's nappy.
He is in the army,
And he is a bit barmy.
He has to be able to jump out of planes,
I think it is safer to get on a train.
He knows how to use a gun,
Which sounds a lot of fun.
My uncle and aunty took me on holiday in the sun,
And we had a lot of fun.
My uncle took me on a boat in the sea,
My aunty said we looked the size of a pea.
      I want to be just like my uncle.

Eliot Newman (9)
Heol-Y-Celyn Primary School

WINTER DAY

The branches hanging on
the glistening trees,
were as bright as a glistening
snowflake.

The breath of the wind
blew the twinkling flakes
flying through the air.

The moor was gleaming with
bright and beautiful sparkles,
in all the gutters across the land
slush as deep as a hole in the pavement.

Matthew Sealey (11)
Heol-Y-Celyn Primary School

SWEET DREAMS

The baby cries,
All through the night,
We do not know
He had a fright!

Mummy soothes
His fevered brow,
That's alright,
It's better now.

Baby knows
His mummy cares,
She will chase
Away his scares.

Sleep in peace
Precious one,
Mummy knows
Your day is done.

Sweet dreams
Little one.

Michaela Evans (9)
Heol-Y-Celyn Primary School

MY DOG

she is the dog you would like to meet
she has some fur upon her feet
she might be ugly
but she's also cuddly
she plays with a ball
with no fuss at all
her wagly tail
it's black, not pale

she has a white patch
she knows how to catch
we have lots of fun
when we're out in the sun
and when it is raining
we do lots of training
how to sit and to beg
until it's time to be fed

she's out in the garden digging a bone
since I've had her I've never been alone
    she is the best
although she's sometimes a pest

Cerianne Owen (10)
Heol-Y-Celyn Primary School

THE EASTER BUNNY

Once I saw an Easter bunny
To me he looked rather funny
He never brought me any eggs
Because I went and pulled his legs

When I woke up I was very sad
But now I know I was bad
I'll make sure I won't do it again
But next year I'll be ten.

Claire Weston (10)
Heol-Y-Celyn Primary School

IT'S SUNDAY

O dear! O dear!
I'm ever so sad.
It's Sunday morning
And the weather is bad.

We get to the track
And what do I see.
A wet and muddy track
Staring back at me.

We wait for the start
15, 5 seconds, off we go.
Got to keep the throttle on.
You just can't go slow.

One more race
It's announced over the mike.
I'm really, really dirty
And so is my poor bike.

O Dear! O dear!
Is all I can say.
I'll pray hard all week.
Please be sunny, the next race day.

Brian Davies (10)
Heol-Y-Celyn Primary School

JUNGLE

On a bright sunny day
The lion pounces at his prey
While the zebras start to run
The lion cubs start having fun
As the eagles start to fly
Rhinos charge at the hunters
That go by
The snake slithers on the ground
While the vultures fly around
The sound of the hunter's gun
Makes all the animals in the jungle
Run.
The hippo swims under the sea
He caught a fish, I'm glad it's not me!
The birds that fly around
Warn the animals on the ground
That hunters are near
Then in jumps a lion and roars
'Never fear.'
The animals are safe once again
Safe from men.

Gabrielle Louise Bunn (10)
Heol-Y-Celyn Primary School

SPRING

When all the winter frost has gone
We start another year,
The springtime sun has heated the ground,
New plants soon appear.

Of all the four seasons,
I like spring the best,
I love to see the green leaves,
And birds make their nests.

Laura Rees (9)
Heol-Y-Celyn Primary School

ENEMIES

I punched,
He ducked.
I narrowed my eyes,
And zipped up my teeth,
That wanted to bite.
I ran,
He shifted.
I crashed into the brick wall,
Blood came pouring.
He rushed up to me,
And kicked me.
I fell,
I rolled in pain,
Across the rough playground.
Everyone was watching!
I'm not a poof!
I'm not going to give up!
This was war!
I wanted to kill him!
I would have . . .

If 'sir' hadn't come *out!*

Jessica Titley (9)
Heol-Y-Celyn Primary School

Music

Music.
Swaying silently, like a breeze.
Rumbling noisily, like a stampede!
Squeaking quietly, like a mouse.
Screeching piercingly, like a barn owl.
Blowing happily, like an elephant.
Beautiful,
Happy,
Sad,
Funny,
Breathtaking.
Music.
Spinning and spinning, like a tornado,
Crying and crying, like a storm.
Blundering clumsily, like a bull in a china shop.
Slow and steady, like a tortoise.
Fast and daring, like a cheetah.
Tired and sleepy, like a sloth.
Music.

Danny Owen (10)
Heol-Y-Celyn Primary School

Valentine's

Valentine's is all about love
Like two birds called doves
You write a card to the person you admire
Bad luck if they put it in the fire
If you're lucky count to two
And maybe she will go out with you
It you're happy you will smile
Even if it's been for a while.

Nathan Evans (9)
Heol-Y-Celyn Primary School

HOUSES

Houses in our street
Stand like soldiers in a row
Chimneys on the roof
Blowing smoke into the sky
Wind blows the smoke
Making it look like
Dancers on the stage.

Houses come in all shapes
Sizes and colours
Curtains at the windows
Move as people look out
To see their gardens full
Of colourful flowers.

Waiting gates ready to be opened
Postmen with their big bags
Full of letters to be pushed through
The mouth of the doors
Lights flickering on and off
Cars lining the road protecting their houses.

Menna Jane Lucas (9)
Heol-Y-Celyn Primary School

MY FISH

The fish is gold
The fish is cold
The fish is wriggly
And it is tickly
The fish is slippery
And it is jumpy.

Louise Walton (9)
Heol-Y-Celyn Primary School

DAVID BECKHAM

David Beckham
David Beckham
Go David

David Beckham
Is the best
David Beckham and the rest
David Beckham
Drinks a few
All night long
With his crew
David Beckham
Missed one goal.
But wait
Now he's scored a goal
David Beckham
And his crew
They all play for
Man U
David Beckham is most liked.
He is married to Posh
Spice.

Amy Louise Jones (11)
Heol-Y-Celyn Primary School

MY BIRD

I have a bird called Spike
Who thinks he is a punk rocker
He sings his song all day long
I think he is off his rocker.

Thomas Hale (8)
Heol-Y-Celyn Primary School

SNOWY NIGHT

A cold winter night
when snow has been falling
like sparkling tinsel
everywhere,
it's like a chocolate flake.

Children playing or even singing
throwing snowballs
building snowmen.

The children were having
great fun but then
the sun came out
and melted the flaky
white snow away.

Sally Webber (10)
Heol-Y-Celyn Primary School

WINTER

Winter has come
This winter day
What will mum do?
She'll shout and pray.

The park is covered with snow,
The children cannot go.

The car's crashed on the ice,
Bit by bit -
It goes crack.

Nicky Hopkins (11)
Heol-Y-Celyn Primary School

MY BIRD DAISY

My bird is yellow and green
With two blue cheeks that are always clean
She flies around the house as quiet as a mouse
She sits in my hair and tries to make a nest
But I still think Daisy is simply the best
She sleeps like a flower
All snug in her bed
I like to smooth her soft silky head
Her claws are quite sharp
She could easily play the harp
When I was eating my tea
Daisy flew over and kissed me

I love my bird Daisy.

Ffion Bunn (8)
Heol-Y-Celyn Primary School

THE LITTLE BOY

There was a little boy,
Who had a little toy,
He went up his nan's to stay,
Where he liked to play,
He went for a walk with the dog,
And came back with a big fat log,
He went to play down the park,
And didn't come home until dark,
And when it was time to go home to dad,
The little boy was so sad.

Joshua Cadwallader (8)
Heol-Y-Celyn Primary School

THE WINTER NIGHT

The winter night had arrived swiftly
Whispering; rustling through the air
Where glittering snowflakes fall everywhere,
Jack Frost had worked his magic
In the frosty, star-filled night.

The winter morning had come gradually
The red gleaming sun shone down
To the cobwebs of rambling rose.

Slush in gutters
Ice in lanes
Frosty patterns
Where hoar frost lay.

Jodie Evans (10)
Heol-Y-Celyn Primary School

BEST FRIENDS

Best friends are always there,
You laugh and cry with, they always care.
I think it's important to have a good friend,
Someone who cares and is there to the end.
My best friend and me go everywhere together.
Shopping, discos, swimming and bowling, wherever, whatever.
My friend is always there for me, when I'm feeling sad.
When I'm lonely and down, when I'm feeling bad.

Emma Raison (9)
Heol-Y-Celyn Primary School

FAIRGROUND

Screaming, shouting, screeching, laughing
Are the sounds I hear.
These noises are so very loud
They are coming from the excited crowds.
People whizzing round and round,
Others going up and down.
The dodgem cars are really fast,
Everyone trying to keep their grasp.
Stalls have sticky candyfloss,
Burgers, hot dogs, ice cream too.
Plenty of games and amusement arcades,
We're all going to have such fun.

Joshua Hawkins (7)
Heol-Y-Celyn Primary School

MY KITTEN

I had a little kitten
Tinker was her name
We spend all day together
Playing little games.
Tinker was a rascal
She chewed up all the mat
Mummy shouted at me
'Where is that naughty cat?'

Nadine Rosenberg (7)
Heol-Y-Celyn Primary School

EARTH AND SPACE

Earth has gravity, Earth has air
and has lots of people there

Earth has lorries, streets and cars
not like boring planet Mars

Space has planets, example, like Mars
and has very, very bright stars
Space has darkness and a few galaxies
Earth has quite a lot of art galleries

Space has stars like the Milky Way
but there is no one to come outside and play.

Sam Fletcher (8)
Heol-Y-Celyn Primary School

NUTS

I like nuts, yes I'm a nutter
Give me lots of peanut butter

If the people ask for cake
Peanut is the one to make

Peanut spread is rich and fine
Don't you take a lot of mine

Peanut butter seems to me
Everything it ought to be.

Kieran Williams (9)
Heol-Y-Celyn Primary School

CARDIFF CITY FC

When Saturday comes I'm up like a lark
I go to watch City at Ninian Park
I collect my ticket and go to the stand
Ready to watch the best in the land

The crowd get excited, up goes the roar
As my team prepare to go to war
The match kicks off
The ball's in the net
'Wow' we haven't played a minute yet

As half time comes
City are winning
I go to the café
For a hot dog with trimmings

The second half starts
We score once more
To make it 2-0
The crowd shout encore

Full time has come
We've won again
It is time to go home
Time for the train

Back at the house
I take a well-earned rest
And think to myself
City are best

Daniel Evans (10)
Heol-Y-Celyn Primary School

THE DAFFODILS

The daffodils
bloom better now
than ever they have before.
Their golden
trumpets
wave on top
of green stalks by
the score.

They know
that today,
is a special day.
Their beauty they
must show.
And tell the
world a secret
that all in Wales
know.

For today is the
feast of Dewi Sant,
it's our
Eisteddfod day.
We'll sing our
hearts out,
raise the roofs!
For all in Wales
today.

Cael Light (10)
Heol-Y-Celyn Primary School

My Dog!

My dog is white,
He doesn't bite.
He waggles his tail when he's happy,
When we give him food he goes wacky.

He is a little Westie
And sometimes gets quite chesty.
Sometimes he wanders out in the street,
And my mother shouts, 'You've got dirty feet!'

My dog is getting on,
And when he does a number 2 - what a pong!
Some of my friends are scared of dogs,
I'm not, I love them.

My dog's name is Taffy,
He's never been in a café.
He runs as fast as light,
I bet he'd give Mike Tyson a fight.

He eats his food in two seconds flat,
And then he goes and lies on his mat.
Sometimes cats come into our garden,
But Taffy's always there to scare them away.
        I love my dog!

Rhys Downes (10)
Heol-Y-Celyn Primary School

SORRY!

Why is the word 'sorry'
So very hard to say?
Your fingers go numb
Your arms go stiff
Your mouth goes very dry.
And even when that little word
Is ready to pop out,
It tingles upon your slimy tongue
Ready to roll out,
Until you have to scream and shout!
'I'm *sorry*!'
And then you run out,
And grumpily stomp up the stairs . . .
Bang, bang, bang!
Then my mum shouts up the stairs -
'Your attitude is awful -
Stay up there and think about what you've done!'
I walk down the stairs and say quietly -
'Mum, I've thought about what I've done -
Can I go out!'
'No, you are grounded, get back up those stairs!'
Sorry!

Nikki Parfitt (10)
Heol-Y-Celyn Primary School

MOTHERS

The truest of
friends
The most loving
and best:
Through trying
years
Have stood
the test;
Ever she's ready
Our troubles to share,
Never once
failing
She's always
there.

Whatever the
problem
She tackles
With zest:
Until the day's
toil be done
she thinks
not of rest;
Working long
hours with no
time to spare,
An angel is
Mother
She's done her
share.

Nathan Thomas (11)
Heol-Y-Celyn Primary School

MY DOG

My dog is brown
She has black stripes
She is smooth
She jumps on me
She licks me
She likes being tickled
She's got brown eyes
Like my dad
She is playful.

Rhianydd Jones (10)
Heol-Y-Celyn Primary School

WAVES

Some waves are big
Some waves are small
But there is one wave
That I like most of all
Splashing, flashing,
Spitting, hissing,
Swishing, whirling,
Twirling, whizzing
Through the rocks
Bashing, thrashing,
Jumping, bumping
And there it goes
Never-ending wave.

Rhiannon Hatter (11)
Llanharan Primary School

COLOURFUL NIGHT

I stare up at the sky,
And wait for the day to go by,
As the sun floats away,
A perfect end to the day.

Not three or four,
But even more,
You are the world's soul,
Never fear the black hole.

You may die
But you still lie,
In my mind forever,
We may never sever.

Emma Bradley (11)
Llanharan Primary School

THE WITCH WITH THE TWITCH

I know a witch
Who has a rotten twitch
She looked in the mirror
And saw a gorilla
The gorilla spoke
She had a stroke
And that was the end
Of the witch
With the twitch

Jade Allen (11)
Llanharan Primary School

ANIMALS

A cheetah can run like the sound of a whip,
A fish can explore a wrecked old ship,
A dog can howl at the moonlit sky,
A skunk can smell, enough to make you cry,
A mouse loves to eat chunky yellow cheese,
'*Stop* that magpie trying to steal my keys!'
A lemur climbs from tree to tree,
A fly is small just like a flea,
A snake slithers to and fro,
An eel wiggles from head to toe,
The active bat comes out at night,
The crocodile's teeth all gleaming and white,
A frog can leap from place to place,
A swan can move with ease and grace,
A bear stands tall, as big as a man,
'The elephants are stampeding, run as fast as you can!'
A horse can gallop as fast as a breeze,
Whales dive deep in the ice-cold water, cold enough to make
                you freeze,
So look after them all,
Don't make them extinct
And please don't wear a coat of mink!

Rhiannon Davies (10)
Llanharan Primary School

THE DEEP BLUE OCEAN

The night before last I was thinking,
I was thinking of the ocean.
The way the waves lap over each other
And how it whistles through the night
And how it feels when it's touched by smooth, small hands.
The glistening water lets sailing ships go through it.
I wonder.
I'll keep wondering.

Ruth Houston (10)
Llanharan Primary School

THE RHONDDA GIANT

The Rhondda Giant was so vain
He thought that the sun rose just to see him.
He was so big-headed
He believed that the stars only twinkled because they saw him.
He was so full of himself
He thought that every girl in the Rhondda should marry him.
He was so confident
He was convinced that the birds sang beautifully just for him.
He was so sure of himself
He thought that the tide sparkled in the sea because he swam in it.
He was so vain
He thought he was the strongest and the most beautiful giant in
                                                    the world.
He was so arrogant
He believed that everyone should gracefully worship him.
He boasted, 'I'm the biggest! I'm the best! I'm a *Super-Giant*!'

Luke W Davies (10)
Llwyncrwn Primary School

THE RHONDDA GIANT

The Rhondda Giant was so vain
He thought that the sun rose just to see him.
He was so big-headed
He believed that the stars shimmered in the dark gloomy sky just
                for him.
He was so full of himself
He thought that every girl fancied and worshipped him to bits.
He was so confident
He was convinced that the birds whistled to him every morning and
                sang him a merry tune.
He was so sure of himself
He thought that the tide would wave to him while he was in the bath in
                the morning.
He was so vain
He thought he was jelly smothered in cream.
He was so arrogant
He believed that everyone worshipped the ground that he walked on.
He boasted, 'I'm the biggest! I'm the best! I'm the *Super-Giant!*'

Sasha Pike (9)
Llwyncrwn Primary School

FROST

Freezing fingers
Robin is sitting in the tree
Other birds flying away
Snowing today
Tingling toes

Michael Hughes (10)
Llwyncrwn Primary School

THE RHONDDA GIANT

The Rhondda Giant was so vain
He thought that the sun rose just to see him.
He was so big-headed
He believed that the stars sparkled only because he was born.
He was so full of himself
He thought that every girl simply found him very attractive.
He was so confident
He was convinced that the birds only flapped their golden wings just for
                                                                                                his delight.
He was so sure of himself
He thought the tide bowed to the land that only he stood on.
He was so vain
He thought he was jelly smothered in a lot of cold cream.
He was so arrogant
He believed that everyone adored the ground that his footsteps trod on.
He boasts, 'I'm the biggest! I'm the best! I'm a *Super-Giant*!'

Mathew Smith (10)
Llwyncrwn Primary School

FROST

Frosty night
Robins whistling with cold.
Other children making snowmen.
Snow comes down then sledges sliding down the hill.
Then it's time to go home for tea.

Scot Taylor (10)
Llwyncrwn Primary School

THE RHONDDA GIANT

The Rhondda Giant was so vain
He thought that the sun rose just to see him
He was so big-headed
He believed that the stars lit up his way
He was so full of himself
He thought that every girl admired just him
He was so confident
He was convinced that the birds sang lullabies to get him to sleep
He was so sure of himself
He thought that the tide was his own special bath
He was so vain
He thought he was as cool as icing on a cake
He was so arrogant
He believed that everyone bowed down and worshipped him at his feet
He boasted, 'I'm the biggest! I'm the best! I'm a *Super-Giant!*'

Craig Hughes (9)
Llwyncrwn Primary School

FROST

Fingers freezing
Roly-poly snowman
Oh it's melting
Slushy snow
Tingling toes.

Adam Pincott, Jesse Bees & Scott Ireland (7)
Llwyncrwn Primary School

THE RHONDDA GIANT

The Rhondda Giant was so vain
He thought that the sun rose just to see him.
He was so big-headed
He believed that the stars shimmered like his own personal jewels.
He was so full of himself
He thought that every girl idolised the ground that he walked on.
He was so confident
He was convinced that the birds migrated to sing just for him.
He was so sure of himself
He thought that the tide rose and fell to give him a bath.
He was so vain
He thought he was a necessity to everyone.
He was so arrogant
He believed that everyone worshipped him.
He boasted, 'I'm the biggest! I'm the best! I'm a *Super-Giant*!'

Phillip Davies (9)
Llwyncrwn Primary School

RAIN

The sky turned black
and it started to rain.
Splish, splash as it hit the windowpane.
Outside I watch people run and hide.
Drip, drop as it falls from the sky
making puddles on the floor.
I hope it doesn't rain anymore.

Kelsey Llewellyn (8)
Llwyncrwn Primary School

The Rhondda Giant

The Rhondda Giant was so vain
He thought that the sun rose just for him.
He was so big-headed
He believed that the stars sparkled especially for him.
He was so full of himself
He thought that every girl adored him.
He was so confident
He was convinced that the birds sang a special song for the
                marvellous him.
He was so sure of himself
He thought that the tide waved to him.
He was so vain
He thought he was king cool.
He was so arrogant
He believed that everyone fell to the ground when they saw him.
He boasted, 'I'm the biggest, I'm the best, I'm a *Super-Giant!*'

Kimberley Homer (10)
Llwyncrwn Primary School

Rain

Rain splashed off my roof and my windowpane.
A flood!
It trickled down the drain.
It fell on the leaves on the trees outside.
It left big puddles.
Dad got splashed.
Children dashed across the streets.

Carmen Joyce (8)
Llwyncrwn Primary School

THE RHONDDA GIANT

The Rhondda Giant was so vain
He thought that the sun rose just to see him.
He was so big-headed
He believed that the stars sparkled in the dark, dark night just for him.
He thought that every girl in the universe loved him.
He was so confident
He was convinced that the birds would only sing a lullaby to him.
He was so sure of himself
He thought that the tide would hit the rocks and make a lovely
                                             sound just for him.
He was so vain
He thought he was as cool as an iceberg.
He believed that everyone thought he was the best of all the giants.
He boasted, 'I'm the biggest, I'm the best, I'm a *Super-Giant*!'

Rachel Leanne Jones (10)
Llwyncrwn Primary School

FROST

Freezing snow
Robin flying
Children throwing snowballs
Snowflakes falling down
Time to go home.

Joshua Smith (8)
Llwyncrwn Primary School

THE RHONDDA GIANT

The Rhondda Giant was so vain
He thought that the sun rose just to see him.
He was so big-headed
He believed that the stars twinkled in the black night sky as his own
                personal jewels
He was so full of himself
He thought that every girl in the whole universe worshipped him.
He was so confident
He was convinced that the birds sang and tweeted only for him to relax.
He was so sure of himself
He thought that the tide rose and fell and made a noise only for him.
He was so vain
He thought he was as tasty as a Christmas pudding covered with cream
And had a little bit of holly on the top.
He was so arrogant
He believed that everyone praised him as if he was a God.
He boasted, 'I'm the biggest! I'm the best! I'm a *Super-Giant*!'

Sarah Bray (10)
Llwyncrwn Primary School

THE DOCTOR

A doctor is blue and white.
He is the autumn seas in a surgery.
A frosty evening.
A long blue gown.
A long, wide, soft bed.
He is the sound of a siren.
The doctor is a bag of blue wrapped sweets.

Tonianne Landsborough (9)
Llwyncrwn Primary School

DOCTOR

A doctor is white.
He is the summer season in a hospital.
A misty evening.
He is a white coat.
A long white bed.
He is the sound of crying children.
A doctor is a sandwich.

Rhys Hain (8)
Llwyncrwn Primary School

LOLLIPOP LADY

A lollipop lady is yellow
She is the summer season on the road
A rainy day
She is a warm waterproof coat
A small coffee table
She is the sound of a car
A lollipop lady is a lime.

Jade Claridge (9)
Llwyncrwn Primary School

A NURSE

A nurse is blue
She is the summer season in a busy hospital
A sunny morning
She is a long ribbon
A long hard bed
She is the sound of an ambulance
A nurse is a blueberry pie.

Sarah Harrison (8)
Llwyncrwn Primary School

PRISON OFFICER

A prison officer is metal grey.
He is the winter season in an office.
A calm day.
He is a dark green pair of jeans.
A green chair.
A heavy door locking.
A prison officer is a green cabbage.

Dale Cox (9)
Llwyncrwn Primary School

CARETAKER

A caretaker is brown.
He is the autumn season in a busy school.
A chilly evening.
He is a fluffy coat.
A cosy long armchair.
He is the sound of a whistle.
A caretaker is a piece of chocolate cake.

Gemma Evans (8)
Llwyncrwn Primary School

FIREMAN

A fireman is red.
He is the summer season in a firework factory.
A cloudy morning.
He is an air mask.
A long sofa with straight arms.
He is the sound of a siren.
A fireman is a burnt sausage.

Wayne Roche (9)
Llwyncrwn Primary School

TV Man

A TV man is black
He is the winter season in side a big factory

He is the cold morning
He is a navy T-shirt
A silver coloured TV
He is the sound of a crackling TV

A TV man is burnt toast

Stephanie Lia (8)
Llwyncrwn Primary School

Shopkeeper

A shopkeeper is green
She is a spring person in a clean shop
A sunny day with fresh air
She wears an overall
A white milky milkshake
A beeping of the till
She is a sweet taste

Bethan Evans (8)
Llwyncrwn Primary School

Love

If you were strawberries I'd be ice cream making you cool.
If you were a thirsty flower I'd be the gardener feeding you.
If you were a pane of glass I'd be a fly flying all around.
If you were the sun I'd be the moon taking your place at night.

Hannah Vaughan (9)
Llwyncrwn Primary School

LOLLIPOP LADY

A lollipop lady is yellow
She is the summer season in a traffic jam
A sunny day
She is a large waterproof coat
A cold bath
She is the sound of cars beeping
A lollipop lady is a yellow lollipop

Ryan Lee (9)
Llwyncrwn Primary School

FOOTBALLER

A footballer is blue and red
He is the autumn season in a football match
A windy day
He is a pair of shorts and T-shirt
A warm bath with bubbles
He is a sound of a roaring stadium
A footballer is a dish full of energy

Liam Richards (9)
Llwyncrwn Primary School

CAR MECHANIC

A mechanic is brown
He is the summer season by a car crash
A grey cloudy day
He is a large black overall
A warm bath
He is the sound of a drill
A mechanic is a beef pasty covered in brown sauce.

Marc Wingrove (8)
Llwyncrwn Primary School

LOLLIPOP LADY

A lollipop lady is yellow.
She is a winter season on a road.
A windy day.
She is a long straight yellow jacket.
She is a long coat hanger.
She is a sound of a car engine running.
She is a huge juicy lemon.

Demi Garwood (8)
Llwyncrwn Primary School

VET

A vet is white
He is the winter season visiting a farm
A stormy day with a biting wind
A warm white sheep's wool coat
He is a white vet's desk in the waiting room
He is the sound of the animals 'woof and miaow'
A vet is vanilla ice cream

Amy John (9)
Llwyncrwn Primary School

ARTIST

An artist is multicoloured
He is the autumn season out in the countryside
He is a windy day
He is a long black shirt
He is a scruffy chair
He is the sound of a bird whistling
An artist is a cordon bleu dish

Shona Pinniger (8)
Llwyncrwn Primary School

DENTIST

A dentist is mint green
He is the spring season in the waiting room
A windy day
He is a long green coat
A big grey chair
He is the sound of a drill
A dentist is a juicy apple.

Amy Ferguson (8)
Llwyncrwn Primary School

CARETAKER

A caretaker is brown
He is the autumn season in a busy school
A windy afternoon
He is a woolly jumper
A swaying rocking chair
He is a sound of a whistling bird
A caretaker is a bar of chocolate

Chelsea Jefferies (9)
Llwyncrwn Primary School

DOCTOR

A doctor is white.
He is spring season in hospital.
A sunny and a cloudy day.
He is a white long coat.
A clean bed.
He is a sound of crying children.
A doctor is a sandwich with bread.

Michael Graham (8)
Llwyncrwn Primary School

LOVE

If you were strawberries
I'd be the sugar to sweeten you up

If you were a thirsty flower
I'd be the water to wet your pretty petals

If you were pane of glass
I'd be a window sill to hold you up

If you were
I'd be glad to love you.

Nia Buckle (10)
Llwyncrwn Primary School

I LOVE YOU

If you were strawberries
I'd be sugar with you all the time
If you were a thirsty flower
I'd be the water for you
If you were a pane of glass
I'd be the fresh air blowing on you
If you were a chipmunk
I'd be running by the side of you

Charlotte Akers (9)
Llwyncrwn Primary School

THE RAINFOREST

R ain is falling to make me grow
A nimals live from bottom to the top
I n this tree the snake and monkey live
N ot any more, it's all cut down
F or woodcutters came, furniture was made
'O h look,' the people cried, 'our homes have gone.'
'R ivers have turned into mud,' one person said
E verything has disappeared
S un has gone down because there is nothing to shine on
T oday it has gone and will never be seen again

Lucy Daunton (10)
Llwyncrwn Primary School

A HAIRDRESSER

A hairdresser is lilac.
She is the summer season in a salon.
A sunny morning.
She is a long dress.
A revolving chair.
She is the sound of a hairdryer.
A hairdresser is a juicy peach.

Lauren Parry (8)
Llwyncrwn Primary School

The Rhondda Giant

The Rhondda Giant was so vain
He thought that the sun rose just to see him.
He was so big-headed
He believed the stars sparkled only for him.
He was so full of himself
He thought that every girl in the universe idolised him.
He was so confident
He was convinced that the birds sang especially for him.
He was so sure of himself
He thought that the tide let him bathe in it.
He was so vain
He thought he was as cool as ice.
He was so arrogant
He believed that everyone lived for him.
He boasted, 'I'm the biggest! I'm the best! I'm a *Super-Giant!*'

Steven Parry (10)
Llwyncrwn Primary School

Love

If you were strawberries
I'd be smooth white cream all over you.
If you were a thirsty flower
I'd be the everlasting water.
If you were a pane of glass
I'd be the window cleaner cleaning you.
If you were the glue
I'd be the paper.

Robert Andrew Powell (10)
Llwyncrwn Primary School

THE RHONDDA GIANT

The Rhondda Giant was so vain
He thought that the sun rose just to see him.
He was so big-headed
He believed that the stars shone in the pitch-black sky
                                like jewels for his eyes only.
He was so full of himself
He thought that every girl bowed before him and worshipped him.
He was so confident
He was convinced that the birds migrated and flew over to sing their
                songs just for him.
He was so sure of himself
He thought that the tide was his bath and personal Jacuzzi.
He was so vain
He thought he was the handsomest giant in the universe.
He was so arrogant
He thought that everyone praised him when they saw him.
He boasted, 'I'm the biggest! I'm the best! I'm a *Super-Giant*!'

Lucas Prosser (10)
Llwyncrwn Primary School

LOVE

If you were strawberries I'd be the sweet sugar on top.
If you were a thirsty flower I'd be the leaves all around you with water.
If you were a pane of glass I'd be the cold water on you.
If you were a sun I'd be the hot air around you.

Gemma Baldwin (10)
Llwyncrwn Primary School

THE RHONDDA GIANT

The Rhondda Giant was so vain
He thought that the sun rose just to him.
He was so big-headed
He believed that the stars shone on him.
He was so full of himself
He thought that every girl fancied him.
He was so confident
He was convinced that the birds were singing at him.
He was so sure of himself
He thought that the tide rose and fell especially for him.
He was so vain
He thought he was as cool as ice.
He was so arrogant
He believed that everyone thought he was the best.
He boasted, 'I'm the biggest! I'm the best! I'm a *Super-Giant!*'

Bethan Griffiths (10)
Llwyncrwn Primary School

LOVE

If you were strawberries
I'd be smothered with milky cream on top

If you were a thirsty flower
I'd be fresh water waiting for you

If you were a pane of glass
I'd be the fly sticking on

If you were ice cream
I'd be the flake.

Andrew Burrows (9)
Llwyncrwn Primary School

THE RHONDDA GIANT

The Rhondda Giant was so vain
He thought that the sun rose just to see him.
He was so big-headed
He believed that the stars glistened just for him
He was so full of himself
He thought that every girl treasured him and adored him.
He was so confident
He was convinced that the birds migrated just to sing to him.
He was so sure of himself
He thought that the tide rose and fell to wake him up in the mornings.
He was so vain
He thought he was as cool as jelly smothered in cream.
He was so arrogant
He believed that everyone thought that he was the biggest and the best.
He boasted, 'I'm the biggest! I'm the best! I'm a *Super-Giant*!'

Joshua Whitfield (9)
Llwyncrwn Primary School

LOVE

If you were strawberries
I'd be the pancake to keep you nice and warm.
If you were a thirsty flower
I'd be the river to give you fresh water.
If you were a pane of glass
I'd be the sun to shine on you all day long.
If you were a bird
I'd be the wings to help you fly.

Jamie Rees (10)
Llwyncrwn Primary School

THE RHONDDA GIANT

The Rhondda Giant was so vain
He thought that the sun rose just to see him.
He was so big-headed
He believed that the stars twinkled in the dark gloomy
                              night sky just for him
He was so full of himself
He thought that every girl in the whole world worshipped him.
He was so confident
He was convinced that the birds sang a sweet lullaby just for him.
He was so sure of himself
He thought that the tide crashed against the rocks just to wake him up.
He was so vain
He thought he was as tasty as jelly smothered in cream.
He was so arrogant
He believed that everyone in the whole universe treasured him.
He boasted, 'I'm the biggest! I'm the best! I'm a *Super-Giant*!'

Carly Watkins (9)
Llwyncrwn Primary School

LOVE

If you were strawberries
I'd be the soil helping you to grow.
If you were a thirsty flower
I'd be the water pouring to give you a drink.
If you were a pane of glass
I'd be the sun shining on you every day.
If you were a teddy bear
I'd be the one who cuddles you every day.

Gareth Carpenter (10)
Llwyncrwn Primary School

THE RHONDDA GIANT

The Rhondda Giant was so vain
He thought that the sun rose just to see him.
He was so big-headed
He believed that the stars twinkled for him in the night sky.
He was full of himself
He thought that every girl fancied him.
He was so confident
He was convinced that the birds sang a sweet tune just for him.
He thought that the tide worshipped him.
He was so vain
He thought that he was the biggest in the Rhondda valleys.
He was so arrogant
He believed that everyone bowed down for him.
He boasted, 'I'm the biggest, I'm the best, I'm a *Super-Giant*!'

Ryan Lloyd Palmer (9)
Llwyncrwn Primary School

THE RAINFOREST

'Where are the trees?' the monkeys cry
'They are all dead,' the woodcutters replied
'Where is the grass?' the antelope shouted
'It is all gone,' the mowers gloated
'Where is the rainforest?' the animals boomed
'It is all gone,' replied the big black baboon
'Maybe it will grow,' the toucan said
Once it has gone it will always be dead
The rainforest was a sacred place
Not anymore, it's a big disgrace

Lloyd Morgan (9)
Llwyncrwn Primary School

THE RHONDDA GIANT

The Rhondda Giant was so vain
He thought that the sun rose just to see him.
He was so big-headed
He believed that the stars sparkled in the blue night sky
                              especially for him
He was so full of himself
He thought that every girl adored the ground that his feet walked on.
He was so confident
He was convinced that the birds whistled a merry tune just for him.
He was so sure of himself
He thought that the tide crashed against the rocks to wake him up.
He was so vain
He thought he was as cool as ice from a fridge.
He was so arrogant
He believed that everyone was born to serve him.
He boasted, 'I'm the biggest! I'm the best! I'm a *Super-Giant!*'

Alexandra Jones (10)
Llwyncrwn Primary School

THE RAINFOREST

The climate is boiling, the rain softly falls.
'Where is my home?' said the sleepy baboon.
'It's gone, gone, gone,' replied the woodcutters.
'Why did you cut it down?' asked the slithery snake.
The woodcutters replied, 'We make furniture.'
'Oh look,' the native people cried, 'our homes have gone.'
They've turned rivers into mud.
The sun has gone because there is nothing to shine upon.
'The forest is dead,' howled the animals.
'This is the end,' sighed the native people.

Laurie Morgan (10)
Llwyncrwn Primary School

THE RHONDDA GIANT

The Rhondda Giant was so vain
He thought that the sun rose just to see him.
He was so big-headed
He believed that the stars glistened in the dark sky for him
He was so full of himself
He thought that every girl worshipped him and they would die
                                                          especially to see him.
He was so confident
He was convinced that the birds sang a different song
                                                    every morning just for him.
He was so sure of himself
He thought that the tide rose and fell in the clear blue sea just for him.
He was so vain
He thought he was as cool as ice in a fridge.
He was so arrogant
He believed that everyone bowed for him every day and night.
He boasted, 'I'm the biggest! I'm the best! I'm a *Super-Giant*!'

Jonathon Stiff (10)
Llwyncrwn Primary School

REFUGEES

I felt so lonely,
As lost as a homeless puppy,
Inside I felt wretched and yucky,
Tired and confused, emotional and sad,
My heart was broken, I thought it was bad.

I saw my world spinning green and blues,
I saw clouds that looked like people I knew,
I saw dead and dying lying around me,
I nearly cried when I saw my bestest friend Vicky - *dead!*

Emma Stafford (10)
Llwyncrwn Primary School

The Rainforest

The rainforest is a huge place
It's a place where all the animals race
If the rainforest is cut down
The animals and natives would surely frown
The rainforest is the animals' home
If it's cut down it will be unknown
If the rainforest is destroyed
Everybody will be really annoyed
If the rainforest is cut down
It would upset everybody in town
The animals are crying, in fear and dread
Because their home - the rainforest is now surely dead.

Tyla Campbell (10)
Llwyncrwn Primary School

Cruel and Unkind

C is for cry
R is for refugees
U is for unkind
E is for experience
L is for lonely

U is for unspeakable
N is for nightmare
K is for kindness
I is for invasion
N is for negotiate
D is for distress

Mathew Binding (11)
Llwyncrwn Primary School

FEAR!

A fter dinner we had to move
F ive thousand people had to go
R efugee - I'd hate to be called refugee.
A t the end of the street I got pulled from Mum and Dad.
I n the train I missed Mum and Dad.
D enmark is where I live now, I was adopted.
  I've got a new mum and dad.

A fraid.
N obody would play with me.
D enmark was a big place - I got lost easily.

F riends, where were all my friends I wondered?
E xcited - because I met my first friend Emma
At the small corner of the house. I cried.
R efugee, I sort of got used to it.
F ive hundred people died.
U nhappy is how I felt,
L onely inside.

Victoria Mary Aldred (11)
Llwyncrwn Primary School

SCARED

S ad and lonely.
C onfused and frightened, tired.
A lso shocked from the war.
R egaining strength I feel better.
E nd of war, fright over.
D ays fly in school

David T J Lacey (11)
Llwyncrwn Primary School

SCARED

S is for sadness and shocked because of the people dying.
C is for confused and my stomach is always churning.
A is for astonished for the people that are still living.
R is for rescuing people.
E is for emotional for the people that are crying.
D is for devastated for the shooting.

Samantha Lia (10)
Llwyncrwn Primary School

REFUGEE

I felt astonished, I had to leave.
I felt nervous and I was very quiet.
I was confused and angry.
I was upset and had stomach burn.
I was homesick and devastated.
I felt like no one liked me.

Mark Slade (10)
Llwyncrwn Primary School

THE DESERT

D ead donkeys lying on the floor
E veryone falls from the wind's roar
S corpions sting and attack
E veryone shouts, 'Let's go back!'
R olling sand crosses the desert floor
T umbleweeds knock men to the floor.

Luke Frater (11)
Llwyncrwn Primary School

REFUGEE

Lonely and lost
and in despair,
fear not children
he'll be there.

Please do not cry
he's up in the sky
he'll help you through
your lonely life.

He'll watch your every move
he'll follow your every step,
because if he did not
we'd be frightened and upset.

Laura Halliday (11)
Llwyncrwn Primary School

ESCAPE OUT

9 o'clock
On the dot
Better be out
Of the country.
Pack your bags
Not a lot
Better be ready for me.
Now
Don't tell your mates.
No making dates.

Paul Morris (11)
Llyncrwn Primary School

Hurt

H ome they never see
U nspeakable people they'll always be
R efugees leave their homes
T hen they're left to die alone.

Clare Morgan (11)
Llwyncrwn Primary School

Sandstorm

Strong
rough sandstorm
whistling, whirling, swirling,
soaring, roaring, powerful blizzard
deadly, desert, isolated, sandy hurricane

Andrew Moore (10)
Llwyncrwn Primary School

Sandy

S un is very hot in the desert
A nd very bright
N ever stay still in a sandstorm
D ry sandy sand
Y ellow sun shining

Joanne Saunders (10)
Llwyncrwn Primary School

SANDY DESERT POEM

D eserts are very hot and steamy.
E ven little deserts are hostile to man.
S trong, whirling, twirling, swirling, blizzards are performed.
E lasticated deserts are very deadly, strong winds would sweep you off your feet.
R aising, swirling, rapid, sandstorms could blind you.
T he blinding sun could pierce your eyes.

Ben Thomas (11)
Llwyncrwn Primary School

REFUGEES

R efugees everywhere, planes bombing us.
E veryone running from the planes, not trusting anyone.
F rightened of the Germans attacking us.
U nspeakable deaths, everywhere there are people dead.
G ermans were stripping us naked and gassing us.
E ndless shooting.
E veryone in pain.
S oon it was all over.

Adam Walters (10)
Llwyncrwn Primary School

REFUGEES

L ost and lonely,
O h no, everyone is gone.
S ilent, nobody there.
T errified that it will come again.

Dominic Hickman (11)
Llwyncrwn Primary School

REFUGEES

We lived in a village
With a roof over our head,
We called it home
But it was only a shed.
We were poor but happy
With all that we had.
As I found out next morning
When things all turned bad.
The floor started shaking,
Concrete falling all around,
Children screaming
To the deafening sound.

The earthquake was a disaster
Everything was lost,
But we thank God
We are safe now,
But counting the cost.
Our home is a sheet now!
Which hangs from the trees,
But we are not called a *family*
We are called *refugees.*

Steven Perkins (10)
Llwyncrwn Primary School

HOSTILE DESERT

The boiling desert days
The freezing desert nights
All those sunny rays
All the sandstorm fights

Katie Murdoch (10)
Llwyncrwn Primary School

A WINGED BIRD

A winged bird far
away and unknown had
wings coloured unlike silver and snow. They
were golden and large, mysterious and bold. A
magnificent sight for the eye to behold.

This bird flew across land and sea, across
chaotic hurricanes, blizzards and raging seas.
Across fiery volcanoes, to other worlds not
known to woman or man. A rainbow high,
crosses the sky wherever this bird may be.

Watch out though, his eyes are brighter than
the sun, if you look directly at them you'll
be as blind as a seedless bun.

Darren Millard (11)
Llwynypia Primary School

THE PARK

The sky is blue, the grass is green
The park is kept nice and clean.
The children playing on the swings.
The ice cream van ding-a-ling-a-lings.
The slide so tall, the climbing frame
All go to make a children's game.
The trees grow up so very tall.
The children look so very small.
People walk their dogs around
Throwing a stick upon the ground.
The dog picks up the stick and barks.
Oh we do have lovely parks.

Stacey O'Flaherty (7)
Llwynypia Primary School

THE MEMORY OF A SOLDIER

It was the eleventh hour of the eleventh day of the eleventh month,
My uncle came around,
Sensibly he gathered my family,
This was unusual, he wasn't usually sensible,
'I'll tell you a story,' he said.
He started his invisible journey to his past,
Of a painful, horrible and terrible memory.

'I probably would be dead if it wasn't for my mate Bill,
He shot the man who almost had me,
For he shot him in his mouth,
His tongue hung on his chin terribly,
I couldn't leave him there,
I tired to be helpful by simply taking him in my arms,
I felt him tremble, it was too late for the sufferer of war.

I heard a noise,
It was a voice,
A wonderful feeling ran through me,
'We've won, the war's over,' a crowd shouted in joy,
The sight of them laughing and hearing their cheers was beautiful.
Suddenly I looked at the dead boy,
I think he was just a teenager,
His young life was grasped away from him,
This I found hard to handle.

So I hope you can recognise what this day means,
So many suffered for us,
And some against.
But a man is a man,
Sides don't matter when people die.
I was nearly one of them,
And even though that man tried to kill me,
The sight of him still runs in my mind,
I wish I could go back and stop him from dying,
Without killing myself.'

Rhys Hopes (10)
Llwynypia Primary School

LITTLE OLD ME

Spiders crawl upon your hand
Snakes slither across the land
A tiny mouse will try to defend
But little old me I'll be your friend

Birds and bees fly round all day
While cows and horses munch their hay
Now the day has come to an end
Another day is just around the bend
But little old me I'll be your friend

Jordan Jones
Llwynypia Primary School

SCHOOL IS...

School is where I go each day,
The work is hard but it's okay.
School is where I learn life's skills,
To earn the money and pay the bills.

School is where I meet my friends,
The fun we have it never ends.
School is where the teachers shout,
And all the kids begin to pout.

School is where I learnt to add,
But reading books drives me mad.
School is where I like to run,
School is lots of work and lots of fun.

Jordan Lee
Llwynypia Primary School

THE BEACH

The waves lapped against my feet,
As I wandered along the shore,
I closed my eyes against the sun's heat,
In the place I will love for evermore.

As I sat upon the golden sand,
Shaded by the swaying palm trees,
I peered across at the distant land,
As my face was kissed by a gentle breeze.

The birds flew overhead,
As the waves crashed upon the sand,
The sky turned the colour red,
And the scarlet spread across the land.

Danielle Gibbs (10)
Llwynypia Primary School

THE THUNDER

The loud and fearsome thunder booms
As it creeps over the sky.
It angrily thuds like a bear
Stamping through the forest.
Fiercely, fearsome, loudly it pounds the sky.
It crashes angrily, fiercely,
Loudly.
The thunder,
Crashes, booms and thuds.
The thunder.

Rhiannan Windsor (10)
Llwynypia Primary School

THE FOG

The fog passes walls and houses.
Slowly travels down chimneys.
Down, down, down 'till it gets
To the blackened, long logs.
It sneaks round the living room
In a ghostly trance.

Jake Jones (9)
Llwynypia Primary School

I ONCE KNEW A DOG CALLED GNIPPER

I once knew a dog called Gnipper;
He dug up a smelly old kipper;
He ate it dead quick and felt very sick;
Over poor old Dennis's slipper.

Jamie Evans & Bobbie Morris (11)
Maerdy Junior School

The Dinosaur

Deathly terrifying T-Rex,
Ichthyosaur's the swimming beasts,
Not all dinosaurs were vicious, carnivorous meat-eaters,
like T-Rex, the king of the dinosaurs,
Some were **O**mnivores, like Gallimimus the runner,
Some were **S**cavengers and hunted in packs, like the terrifying
Velociraptor, who'd split your stomach and eat you while you were still alive.
And last of all we come to the peaceful herbivores, who'd only eat plants, but they could still step on you,
Unlike the birds, they didn't survive the giant comet,
They were **R**ulers but they are now extinct, goodbye great beasts,
I loved you all.

Calvin Ben Williams (11)
Maerdy Junior School

Groovy Girls

G roovy girls are great
R un around with a mate
O ver the garden wall
O n top of the waterfall
V alentine's day is when boys come out to play
Y ou love me so I love you too.

Emma Louise Kinson (11)
Maerdy Junior School

WET COAT

One miserable wet day
a coat hook stood up to say
these wet coats
are making me sneeze
take it away
and bring back a summer breeze.
Where children don't need their coats to play
keep it going at least till May.

Rebecca Podmore (10)
Maerdy Junior School

A KINGFISHER

A large beak;
A tiny wingspan;
A fish eater;
A swift glider;
A fish nibbler;
A meat eater;
A good singer;
A lump of feathers.

Martyn Jones & Ieuan Wilding (11)
Maerdy Junior School

THE HILLS OF BRECON

The hills of Brecon are very cold.
The cars fly by, not a care in the world.
The sheep graze the lush green grass.
Trees older than humans live there.
Farmers live there all their lives.
They live in old brown farmhouses.
Small they are but not wet or cold.

Philip Jason Thomas (10) & Kyle Osborne (11)
Maerdy Junior School

MY FAVOURITE ANIMAL

My favourite animal is a horse because I can ride as fast as lightning.
My favourite animal is a dolphin because I can ride the waves.
My favourite animal is a dog because it's cute and cuddly.
My favourite animal is a bird because it soothes my head when I hear its song.
My favourite animal is a cat because its warm fur makes me
feel relaxed.

Sarah Harris (11) & Chloe Light (10)
Maerdy Junior School

MY FAVOURITE SPORT IS FOOTBALL

My favourite sport is football,
Because it's action-packed.
You've got to try and get the ball,
And kick it past the wing attack.

My favourite sport is football,
Because I like to play.
It's fun, it's cool so come and join,
So come and play.

My favourite sport is football,
Because we usually win.
We'll win and win and win the cup
Until we sing.
My favourite sport is football.

Maria Marling (10)
Penygawsi Primary School

WHAT IS BLUE?

Blue is the seagulls
Standing on the edge, squawking.
Blue is the sea
Swaying and dashing
From side to side on a stormy day.
Blue is the sky
With clouds floating by.

Katherine Houghton (8)
Penygawsi Primary School

SUMMER SUN

Flowers! Flowers! Everywhere,
People come to stand and stare.
Holidays to sunny places,
Children join in running races.

Chocolate ice cream melting fast,
Forget the coldness from the past.
Summer holiday nearly gone,
Everybody sings a song.

That's summer sun for us, *yes!*
That holiday was the best I guess.
Back to school,
The holiday was really cool!

Bridie Williams (11)
Penygawsi Primary School

SNOW

Twinkling snowflakes falling softly to the ground,
Silently laying a cold blanket over fields and roads,
Snowmen staring over hills at the twinkling stars,
Owls are hooting, hawks are swooping for their nightly meal,
Daytime robins, chirping sweetly by their kettle nests.

Claire Thomas (9)
Penygawsi Primary School

WALES

I live in a country - its name is Wales
The capital is Cardiff that we all know
Everyone comes to visit this place
Over and over again

A country called Wales, it's the land of song
So everyone comes here to sing along
Come back every year to visit us once more
This is our country called Wales

There's many lovely places to go and stay
There's beaches and there's castles to look at today
In the hills and the valleys you can go and play
Every night and day

A country called Wales, it's the land of song
So everyone comes here to sing along
Come back every year to visit us once more
This is my country called Wales

Alexander Davies (10)
Penygawsi Primary School

RED

Red is a delicious strawberry
Red is a shiny postbox
Red is a juicy apple
Red are my metal toy cars
Red is a warm woolly jumper

Thomas Morgan (8)
Penygawsi Primary School

MY CLASS

My class, my class
Do you work
Put you pen down
In my class

My class, my class
Finish your Maths
Hurry your English
In my class

My class, my class
Do a handstand
And a roll
In my class

My class, my class
Go out to play
Have lots of fun
In the playground
       My class

Francesca Ward (11)
Penygawsi Primary School

SNOW

Cold snow melting
Round snowman leaning
Red robin singing
Green Christmas tree waiting
Wet snowflakes falling
On a winter day

Harvey Moisey (8)
Penygawsi Primary School

IF

If my dad were a dog
he'd be a boxer dog
because he's big and strong.

If my dad were a bird
he'd be an eagle
squawking above me.

If my dad were a colour
he'd be sky blue
because he's always wearing blue.

If my dad were a plant
he'd be a daffodil
making everybody around him happy.

Matthew Giles (8)
Penygawsi Primary School

THE THING I WANT

I want a bike, Mum
I want a bike, Mum
Christmas is coming
Christmas is coming
You never know what you will get
You might have a dog, a bike
Or maybe a new house

Christmas is here, what have you got?
I've got a bike, Mum
It's brand new, Mum
Thanks, Mum, you're the best mum
I've got what I always wanted.

Stella Tsouknidas (11)
Penygawsi Primary School

BOXING

Boxing is a great sport.
Hits them where you never thought.
Uppercut, left jab in the face,
Ooh my gosh,
In the stomach, in the arms, in the face.
In the nose, in the arm, uppercut
Down in the drain goes his blood.
Ding, ding! So the match is halfway through,
The man in red is not giving up yet.
So the next round has begun.
The crowd have gone wild,
The weather is so mild.
The match is nearly over now,
But he's got to win the featherweight.
The match is over.
It's a big, oh how great.
He's celebrating now with sweat and water in his mouth.

Matthew Evans (11)
Penygawsi Primary School

SPRING

Lambs hopping here and there,
Children prancing everywhere.
Daffodils starting to grow,
While the snow melts very slow.

St David's Day is coming up,
Try and win the golden cup.
Write poems, draw pictures, so,
If you lose you'll be full of woe.

Sports day comes once a year,
Everyone should join in at Penygawsi right here.
I love spring very much,
'Cause my rabbits aren't stuck in their hutch!

Rachael Shaw (11)
Penygawsi Primary School

CATS

I have two cats
Called Millie and Mollie
They're really cute
And really jolly

In spring
They play with the butterflies
And sit down to watch
The birds as they fly

Mollie is black and white
With little cute eyes
She's a real monkey
When she plays with my dad's ties

Millie is also black and white
With a silky black tail
Her body is elegant
And rips my dad's e-mails.

I love my cats very much
Especially when they purr
I will never forget, no never
Their silky black fur.

Claire Scowcroft (10)
Penygawsi Primary School

TEACHERS

Mr Pearson:
>A spiky-haired dude,
>Who's good at every sport,
>He's a very good teacher,
>And he's not at all short.

Mrs Bailey:
>She's always got a headache,
>'Cause her class is very loud,
>But she's very good at teaching,
>So she should feel proud.

Mrs Gibbs:
>Extremely good at yelling,
>When someone's made a noise,
>I wouldn't be surprised,
>If she ever lost her voice.

Stuart Wilby (11)
Penygawsi Primary School

RC CARS

Around, around, around goes the cars on the track,
To get your name on the plaque.
Around, around, around we go,
Crashen, smashen, and going slow.

Smash, smash, smash we all crash,
Crash, crash, crash, we all smash.
I win the race,
I'm in first place.

I'm on the plaque,
And that's a fact.
The car that came last,
Wasn't that fast.

Justin Morden (11)
Penygawsi Primary School

TEACHERS

Mr Pearson
    Mr Pearson is so cool,
    He's the best in all the school.
    He's really sporty,
    And all his boys are really naughty

Mrs Bailey
    Mrs Bailey likes PE,
    Doesn't like Science
    But loves her tea.
    She broke her car and lost her keys.

Mrs Gibbs
    Mrs Gibbs she supports Hibs,
    Played rounders and broke her ribs.
    Mrs Gibbs is really cool,
    She beats Mr Pearson in our school.

Carl Hawkes (11)
Penygawsi Primary School

IF

If my mum was a bird
She'd be a woodpecker
Pecking on the trees.

If my mum was an animal
She'd be a gerbil
All precious and white.

If my brother was an animal
He'd be a lion
Because he's bossy.

If my dad was a reptile
He'd be a lizard
Because he swims and jumps about.

Kimberley Hawkes (7)
Penygawsi Primary School

IF

If my sister was an animal
she'd be a monkey,
jumping around everywhere.

If my brother was a fish
he'd be a shark,
he has sharp teeth to bite.

If my mum was a tree
she'd be an oak,
she stands still most of the time.

Sam Griffiths (7)
Penygawsi Primary School

IF

If my cousin was an animal
she'd be a tabby cat
all kind and loving
but fights with her baby brother.

If my cousin was a colour
she'd be sunshine yellow
all bright and shiny.

If my mum was a bird
she'd be a flamingo
all pink and proud.

If my mum was a fish
she'd be a cod
silver and glittery.

Bethan Harrison (7)
Penygawsi Primary School

IF

If my mum was a book
she'd be an encyclopaedia
telling me all the things I need to know.

If my mum was a plant
she'd be a Venus Flytrap
all snappy and weird.

If my mum was an animal
she'd be a snail
all slow and steady.

Daniel Halford (9)
Penygawsi Primary School

IF

If my dad was an animal
he'd be a giraffe
because he's tall.

If my sister was an animal
she'd be a cat
because she crawls and miaows.

If my sister was a colour
she'd be yellow
because she smiles.

If my grandad was an animal
he'd be a dinosaur
because he's fat.

Jamie Sheppard (7)
Penygawsi Primary School

IF

If my dad was a puppy
He'd be a cocker spaniel
All cuddly and cute.

If my dad was a flower
He'd be a sunflower
Big and yellow.

If my dad was a book
He'd be a dictionary
Telling me my spellings.

Sophie Hughes (8)
Penygawsi Primary School

IF

If my favourite cousin was a dog
She'd be a Labrador
Lively, but loving and sloppy.

If my favourite cousin was a colour
She'd be the colour pink
All bright and colourful.

If my favourite cousin was a bird
She'd be a flamingo
All pink and proud.

If my favourite cousin was a plant
She'd be a sunflower
All bright and pretty.

Alexandra Lamb (7)
Penygawsi Primary School

RED

Red is the tasty icing on a cake.
Red is the smelly socks in my drawer.
Red is the metal boat out on the sea.
Red is a juicy big apple.
Red is a shiny ruby.

Thomas Wilton (8)
Penygawsi Primary School

IF

If my dad was a dog,
he'd be a sheepdog.
He'd be fast and strong.

If my dad was a bird,
he'd be a robin.
He'd fly in the freezing snow.

If my dad was a colour,
he'd be bright blue.
He'd brighten up the room.

Thomas Rees (9)
Penygawsi Primary School

WHAT IS BLUE?

Blue is the splashing waves on the rocks
Blue is the sky on a sunny day
Blue is the pansies nodding their heads
Blue is a teddy all cuddly and soft
Blue is bluebells making noises

Lauren Bowkett (7)
Penygawsi Primary School